P9-CRS-406

GREECE TODAY

GREECE TODAY

One More Dark Page in Mankind's History

Enas Hellinas

Exposition Press   *New York*

ST! BONAVENTURE LIBRARY
ST. BONAVENTURE N Y

DF
833
.H45

EXPOSITION PRESS INC.

50 Jericho Turnpike   Jericho, New York 11753

FIRST EDITION

© 1971 by Exposition Press. *All rights reserved, including the right of reproduction in whole or in part in any form except for short quotations in critical essays and reviews.* Manufactured in the United States of America.

0-682-47232-8

228052
3994593

APR 4 '75

MAY 18 '64

*Dedicated to all those who have fought and suffered
for an ideal that has made their country
and themselves immortal*

E. H.

CONTENTS

GREECE TODAY

APRIL 21, 1967

Midnight, the twenty-first of April, 1967, a few days before the scheduled general elections. For some time Greece had been through a turmoil, foreign to the Greek character. There was a cause, there was a reason created for the change. The conspiracy, admittedly enough, was laid ten years ago—to be ready whenever needed and now was the time—under cover of night.

Democracy has not died in Greece—and never will die! The fanatics who tried to kill democracy should have known this by merely looking at the history of their country. Their mistake was that they did not understand what they were looking at was the spirit of their own country.

The late night swingers
were dragging their feet, making their last rounds.
The lights were blinking at the crossroads.
A strange silence was spread around
I remember, when suddenly
the sound of roaring chains
filled the empty space everywhere.

I stopped at the corner to see.
Soldiers! Soldiers on tanks, on trucks!
"What is it?" I asked myself.
Somebody must be kidding.
They were running to the Parliament
filling up the squares.
Isn't that what the SS did?
Nobody could understand, some thought
a game was going on.

That night I still remember—
the night of the "bloodless coup,"
so called, so advertised, so justified.
Hellas entered its darkest era
April the twenty-first.

11

That dawn, I remember,
was meant to bring an aura
to bloom the flowers and excite the people;
to fill up their hearts with hope and love.
That dawn and that aura were to carry
the mandate of freedom that soon was to come.
That day was not meant to become
the most ill-omened day.

That day, the sun rose too late
in a sky that was no more blue.
That day, the boats were rocked and wrecked
in an angry and roughened sea.
That day, the people woke up from a bad dream
in a "New Order" of things to be.
A "New Order"
that needed no parliament or deputies;
no education or teachers.
A "New Order"
that sent people on vacation and to "surgery."
The whole nation—
A "New Order"
that dismissed its officers, inviting nothing
but humiliation.
That day the new "firmani," or law, dictated:

No freedom of speech or gathering.
No music, singing or even thinking
no murmuring or chatting, not even spitting—
it might be of disgust.
That day, how, why, from where, I don't know,
the New Order was established
But one day I will find out,
not for revenge or hate but I just want to know—
I want to know more about friends and enemies
that day—
The *most ill-omened day.*

CALL ME "SPIOUNOS"

"Spiounos" is an informer. He is paid relatively little, but he does a lot of harm to innocent people. He is slightly sadistic, very malicious, a jealous and revenge-seeking person. This is because he has not been able to accomplish anything significant in his life. "Spiouni" is the plural of "spiounos," and there are a lot of them nowadays in Greece. The present governmental scheme makes ample use of them and everyday encourages similar behavior by others.

I get paid, my friend,
I get paid for "being around."
But I don't know what
you may call that—
all I know is only "that."

If I hear you saying
you don't like the "brass,"
If I see you looking down
at the green grass—don't hope.
If I touch you and you move away,
Oh! my friend,
there is no doubt
you're in big trouble.
Oh! ya, indeed you are.

If I "smell" that your movements
don't look right to me,
If I taste your bitterness
when you spit around;
If I sense that your mind is upset one day,
and above all,
If I simply thought that,
Oh! my friend,
somehow
I just don't like you

'cause
you're short or tall,
fat or thin,
your face is grim, or
you laugh too much,
your clothes are good
and you don't give a damn,
or
a girl is around who
likes you.
Oh! my friend,
for any of these reasons
and a million more
I can tell you right now
and don't take me wrong,
you're in
big trouble.

Don't ask the people
who I am
Don't you know
that nobody talks
but the eyes, the
sky and the blue sea?
That's where I can't see—
not even the tourists—these colorful people.
"It's so nice and lovely," they say,
"So quiet, so peaceful
and pretty. Look at the ruins."

Isn't that what the people would like to see?
Oh! yes, my friend,
that's my assignment—
to keep them happy
and tell my "liaison"
what is going on.
My name, you asked?

Well, just call me "Spiounos."
Call me "Spiounos."

It is as simple as that.
I listen to what you say
and get my pay.
I am a social asset
in this new situation;
I send a lot of people on "vacation."
They don't have to pay a thing.
With a little "surgery" and little wisdom
a lot can see the islands
and lose their freedom.

I know one day—
maybe not too long from now—
I may lose my assignment.
There may be no need for it;
I may even be reborn.
I feel so ashamed of myself and
wish from the bottom of my heart that
people no more would call me "Spiounos."

CALL ME "LIAISON"

"Liaison" means "connection," or a sort of public relations man. However, in the circumstances under which Greece is governed today (in 1970–since April 21, 1967) "Liaison" means "spiounos" at a higher level. The present governmental scheme has installed such "liaison" officers in all significant organizations such as banks, public utility firms, corporations and others. Their purpose is to guard their masters against any potential anti-junta movement. Therefore, job security is a funny joke in Greece.

"Hellas Hellinon Christianon" is a governmental slogan suggesting that Greece is or must be a "country of Greek Christians." The irony is that Greeks or Hellines Christians today are suffering as the Christians suffered under the Romans in the past. One wonders whether, in order to survive, he should be a Christian, a Roman or a contemporary "soul reformer."

I am a big fat "liaison,"
so they call me.
I've been recently appointed
to this new assignment.
It is, they say,
a new innovation; the best of all with no confinement.

I sit on my butt and
think in depth
What John said, what Mary did.
All these serious things and many more
must be controlled if
"Hellas Hellinon Christianon"
is to progress a bit at all.

I sit on my butt and
smoke and play with my guesses.
What my "spiouni" will crop for me today.
I must not forget
I am the "liaison" and even more;

17

I supervise them all, and see
how the business is run.
As a matter of fact
there is a lot of fun
in this new innovation of "liaison";
it just puts everybody on—it even turns me on!

Today I heard, in the line of duty, that
people are happy.
They don't talk or smile,
not even some grumbling; strange, nothing at all goes on.
They only look at each other, but
my suspicious mind discovers it all.
It is the 21st, the most glorious day of all!
People of Athens, you have a chance
to show the world. We fight them all—
liberties and civil rights, the European Council,
Democracy above all!
We are here to stay,
people of Athens, and make a stand
against our enemies—our own people.
If Franco has made it, why can't we?

I am a big fat "liaison,"
I am here to stay
and improve the relations
of my masters with the public.
To me "PAPADOC" or "PAPADOP"
it is the same POT.

I am a big fat "liaison,"
so they call me.
What John said, and Mary did
are all together my main thought.
I spend my day
enjoying myself with intimate news
that my "spiouni" bring to me.

My salary is as fat as I am
and all get fatter, and fatter.
It helps if you bend and flatter.

I confess to myself and to all of you.
Oh! 21st of April, how bright of you.
Will you stay forever?
I like the innovation,
your subsidy, the best of all;
it turns me on
when you call me "liaison."

WHY DO YOU TORTURE ME?

"Bouboulinas" Station is the police headquarters in Athens. There the most severe torture takes place. The terrace is used to threaten prisoners by fall. A small room on the terrace—in complete darkness—is used for isolation. In the basement and on various floors there are also rooms which are used for torturing the prisoners.

"Dionysos" is another police station of torture. The area, located near Athens, is also a tourist attraction but this "show" is not for foreign exchange.

There are many police stations in Greece and their number has been dramatically increased during recent years—they want to make sure they can handle all the people, royalists and democrats.

You knocked on my door early this morning
and told me you had orders
to take me to the security police
at Bouboulinas Station. Alas!
At Bouboulinas Station.

Oh! my friend, my brother, oh you!
Why are you beating me so hard?
What have I done to you or to your masters?
Is it because I love freedom?
I understand you have your orders.
You can't stop me from going ahead.

You beat the soles of my feet.
The swelling broke even my shoes
but someday, I'll walk on my knees, or
even in a wheelchair you'll see
you can't stop me from going ahead.

You wrung and twisted my arms and
hanged me from my feet.

You kicked me on my back—I was too tall for you before, yet,
I understand you have your orders.
You can't stop me from going ahead.

You pulled my hair and
smashed my head on the wall but
my thoughts remained free.
Your punches didn't hurt me at all—I felt sorry for you
with your wooden planks, metal wires and rubber clubs.
You can't stop me from going ahead.

You took me to the terrace
at Bouboulinas, at Dionysos and elsewhere
and threatened me from the height.
You threw me in the small room on the cold concrete,
without food or water.
You can't stop me from going ahead.

You bound my hands and feet
there on the bench at the top.
You tried even to rape me—to take my manhood away.
You gave blows on my genitals—to make me impotent.
You dropped me on the floor for many days.
You can't stop me from going ahead.

You took off my toenails and
with cigarettes burned my fingernails.
You even staged a mock execution
and tortured me with water drops on my brow.
You hit me everywhere, I spat blood from mouth and ears.
You can't stop me from going ahead.

You tortured me with "Falanga,"
Crippling my legs, breaking my neck
even without any official charges.
You kept me for months in the dark.
I cannot tell whether it is day or night
You can't stop me from going ahead.

You stuffed my mouth with a urinated rag,
and made me eat human waste and
run naked in the frozen rain.
You put me in the cold dark dungeon and sent me to exile
on islands that tourists don't go to see.
You can't stop me from going ahead.

You threw me off the boat
in the middle of the night in the open sea.
You said I tried to escape—
what irony! You thought you won!
You only got rid of my body, not me.
You can't stop me, my spirit, from going ahead.

MY COUNTRY IS ON SALE

The Prime Minister of Greece, in a statement made for the new year (1970), said, among other things:

Our country's life is peaceful and undisturbed; our monetary stability is undeniable; our national income is increasing . . . and Greek and foreign capital investments are expanding steadily.

As a matter of fact, more steadily than anything comparable to this situation. About three hundred foreign firms have established branches in Greece during the last three years. Business is good. The question is, for whom?

My country is on sale
to all foreign concerns,
for the sake of survival
against all domestic and foreign rivals.
Come on all you sharks,
and tear apart your share.

My country is on sale
to all of those who know
how to wheel and deal,
how to promise millions,
how to raise the standards,
and above all—
How to profit millions.

My country is on sale.
All foreign concerns
send in experts and executives,
managers and proprietors,
technicians, agents, and
please don't forget your advisors.

ST. BONAVENTURE LIBRARY
ST. BONAVENTURE. N. Y.

There is a lot of bread to feed all of you
in this country of beauty and few strong men.

My country is on sale.
No sweat—don't invest;
a promise only will suffice.
In this world of enterprise,
an official will cut the ribbon, I bet
and business will begin to rise—
skyrocket, like the foreign debt.

My country is on sale.
I see resources moving away;
I see youngsters staying away.
I hear this country is all rocks, so poor
but very scenic—what tourists like,
yet wonder as I am told.
Three hundred new establishments from abroad
in just three years
since the "New Order" came along,
and all are there to stay, they say.
I wonder, is there a God to Whom to pray?

My country is on sale—
peacefully and undisturbed,
stable money, rising GNP
the Prime Minister said to be.
Difficulty there isn't going to be
with the innovation of economic infiltration.
Be a little patient and read
the *Foreign Investor's Guide*—a luring device.
I lose all my pride
when I think what a shame
insecurity and thirst for fame can claim.

My country is on sale
to all foreign concerns

which have the "know-how"
of turning stones to fleeing profits.
The "New Order" and
the *Foreign Investor's Guide*
will tell you with pride,
and quite frankly,
the knack of selling your own blood.

My country is on sale.
Like in the past,
you, Mr. Executive,
extract all you can fast. Just
like in the past
all the marbles flew abroad.
Only Acropolis was left alone and
one more thing will now remain with the ruins—
The Spirit.
Spirit and ruins are inseparable twins!
The true lovers of this earth
that now is on sale.

RETURN TO THE HOMELAND

I returned to my homeland
after years of absence
and saw nothing but strangers
wandering the streets and the squares.

I let my thoughts free
to follow the strangers
lest my fearful curiosity, if known,
would scare them away.

Alas! There is no answer to my questions—
Why? What is going on?
Where are the laughs?
Where are the noise makers?
Where are the arguments on politics, on sports—the blood of their
    hearts?
Where are the girl teasers?
Where are the couples to chat at the corners?
Where are THE PEOPLE?

I don't feel them at all.
I see only their shadows—so close!
But can't touch them, they're too far away.

Years ago, I remember like a bad dream
the boots of the foreign troops that broke
the silence of the night.
Their grim faces spread the fear around then
as now, some years later, when the world is meant to be free.
The boots of the local troops break
the same silence, but the pain is there, in their hearts.
They are grim from sorrow of what they must do.
They are the sons of their mothers and fathers,
they are brothers of their own brothers.
They have to betray them all
for an empty cause of a handful of lackeys.

Oh! poor Hellada, when will the sun
rise for you again?

I returned to my homeland
and wandered the streets.
I let my thoughts free.
Alas! There is no answer to my questions—
Where are THE PEOPLE?
To feel them all
I saw but shadows—so close, so far away!

I returned to my homeland only to see
how grim their faces, how silent the night,
how great the fear, how misty the tears have all become.

Oh! poor Hellada, when will the sun rise for you again?

DATE DUE

HIGHSMITH 45-220

3 3226 00071 1731

U/S.

3 3226 00071 1731